STRESS BUSTERS

COLORING BOOK FOR ADULTS

RUCHI BHARGAVA

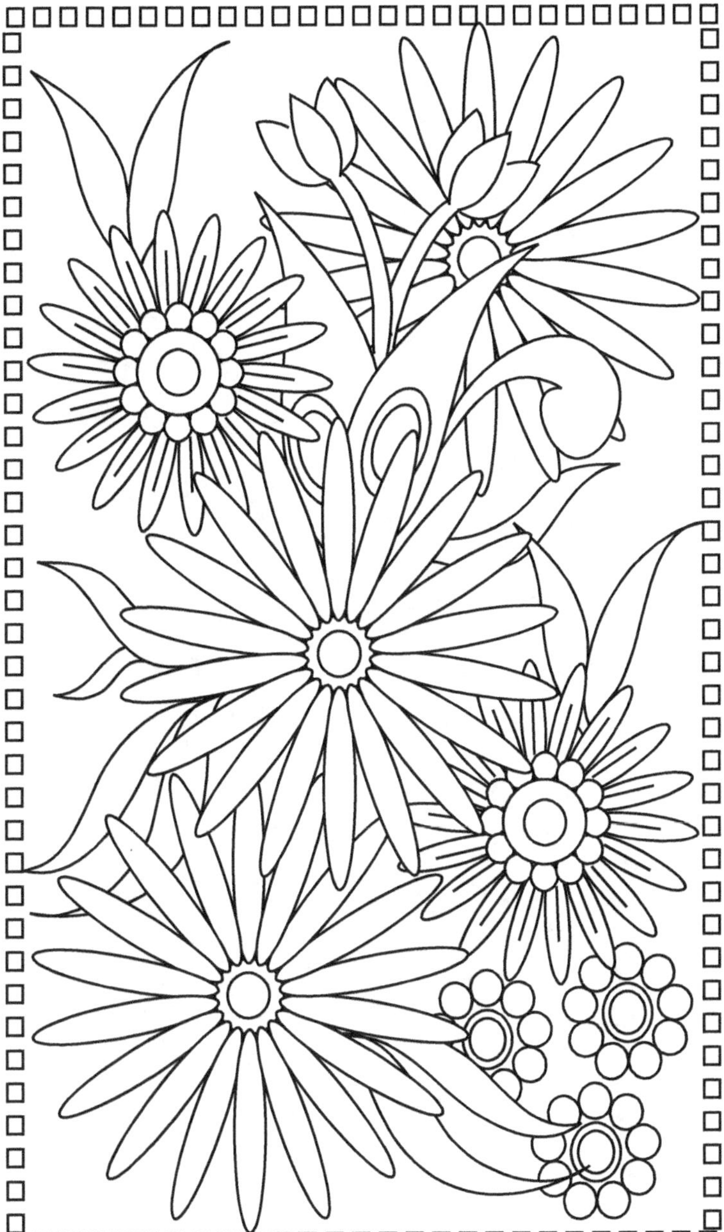

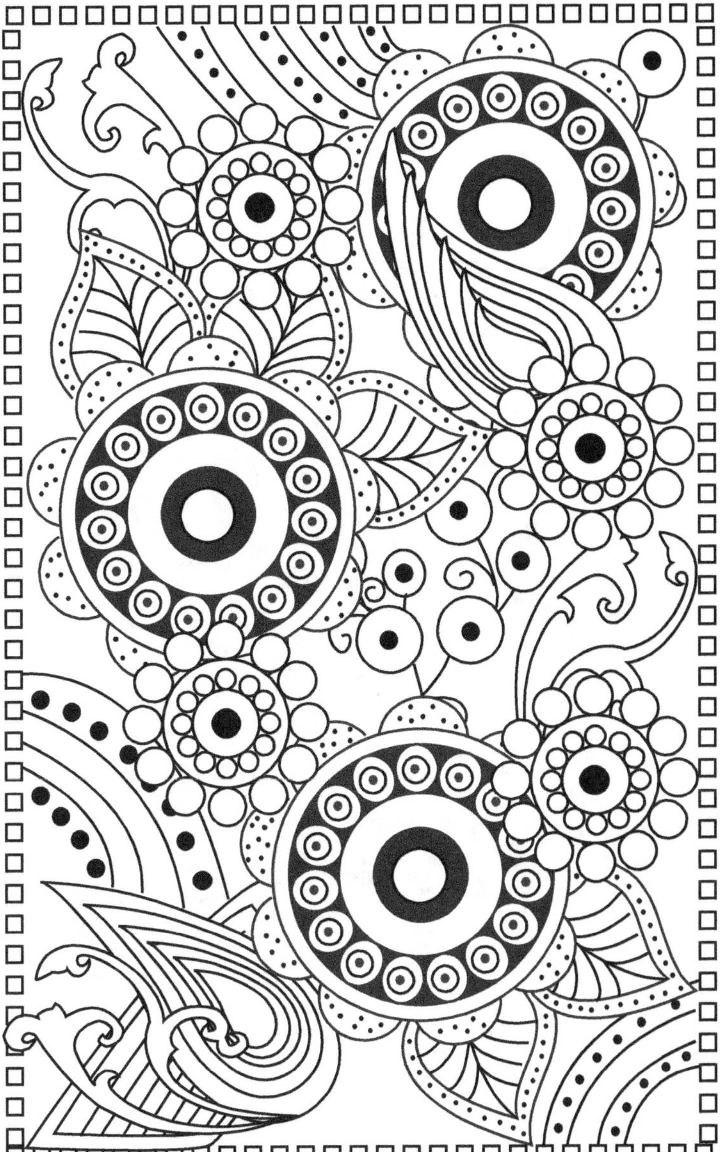

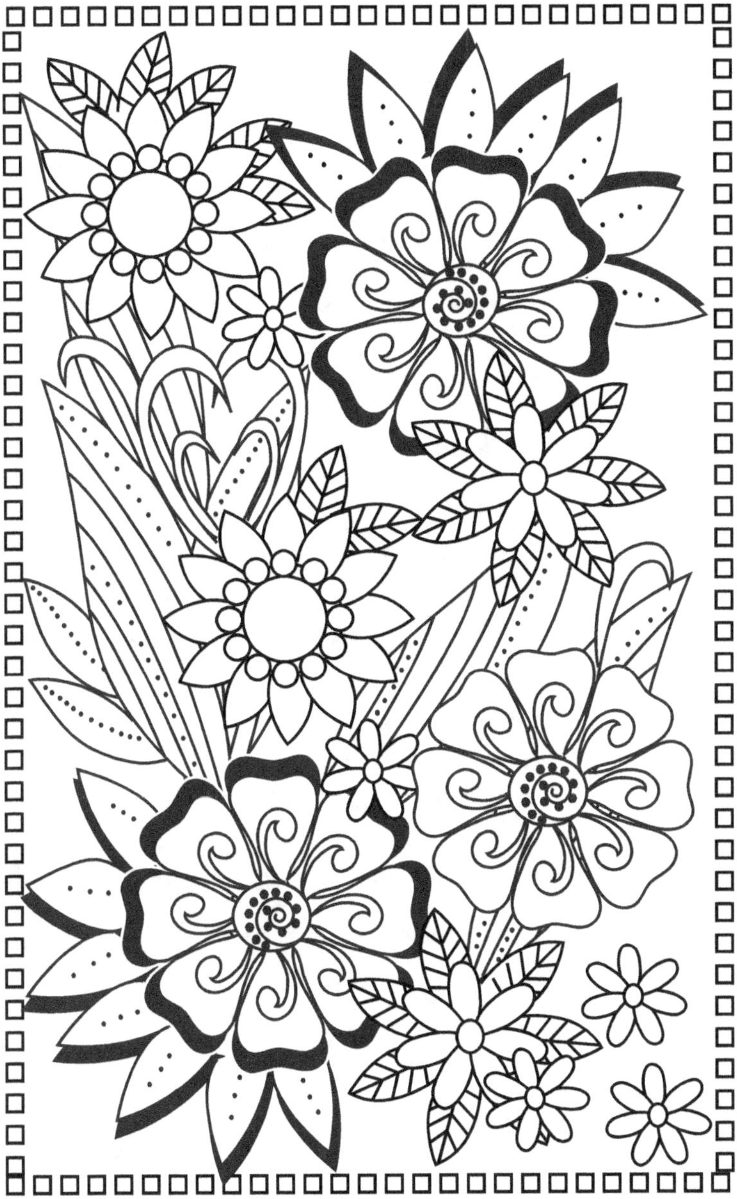

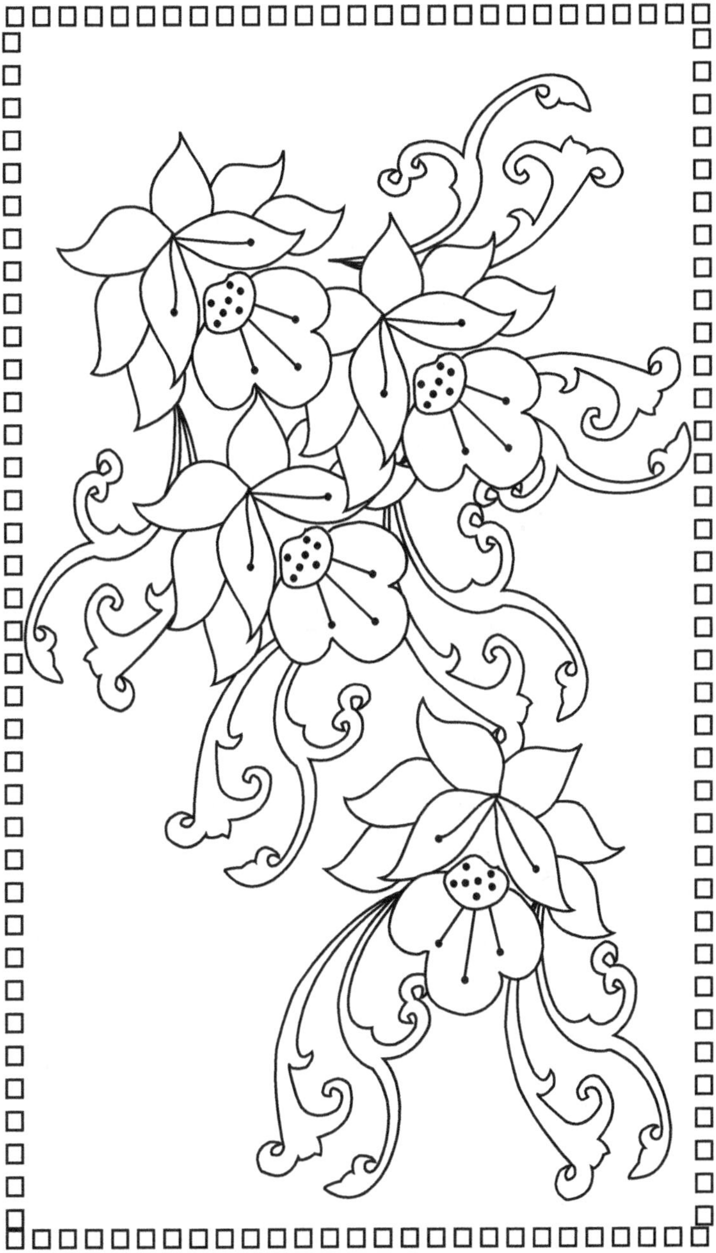

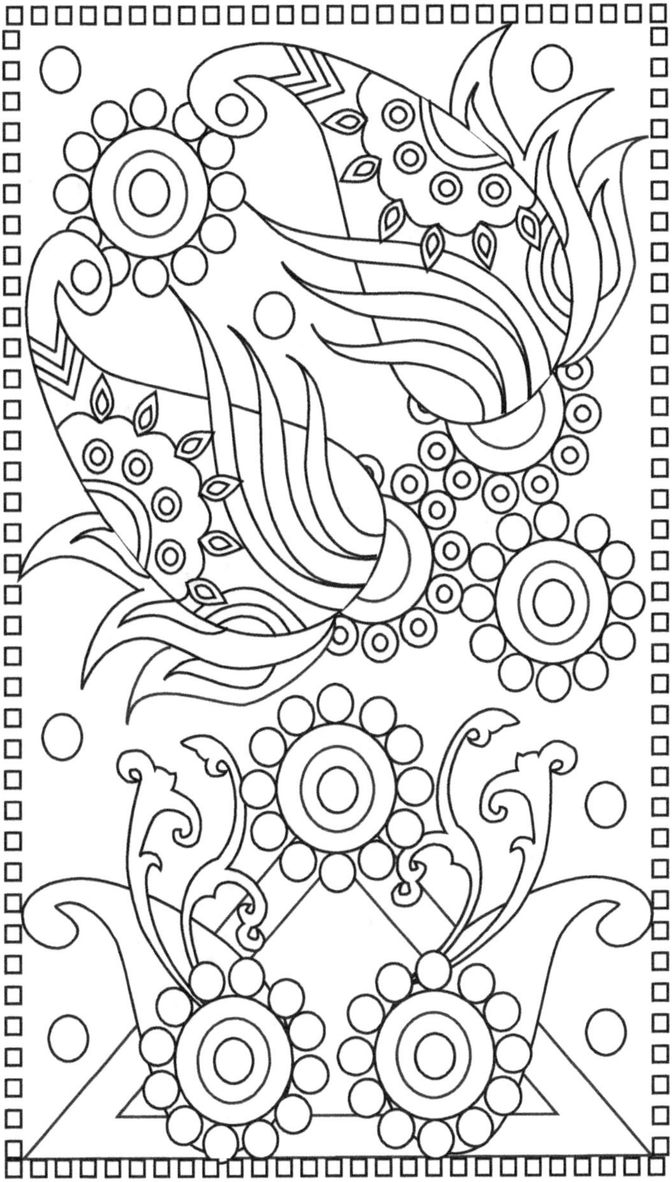

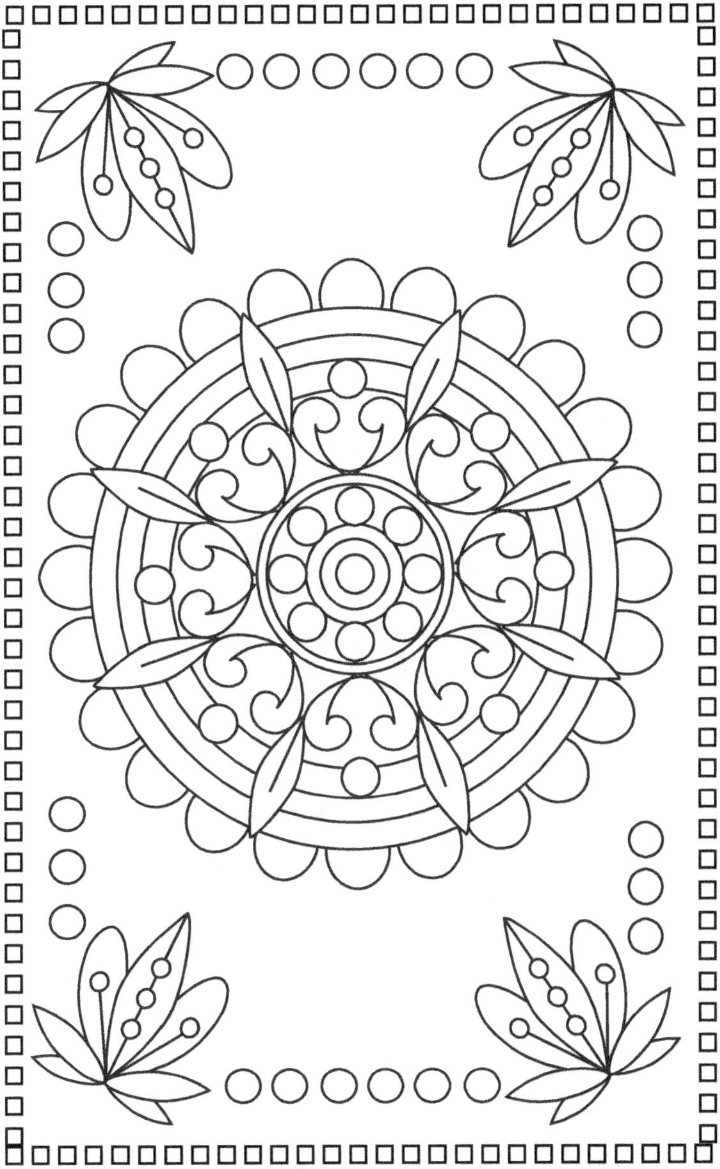

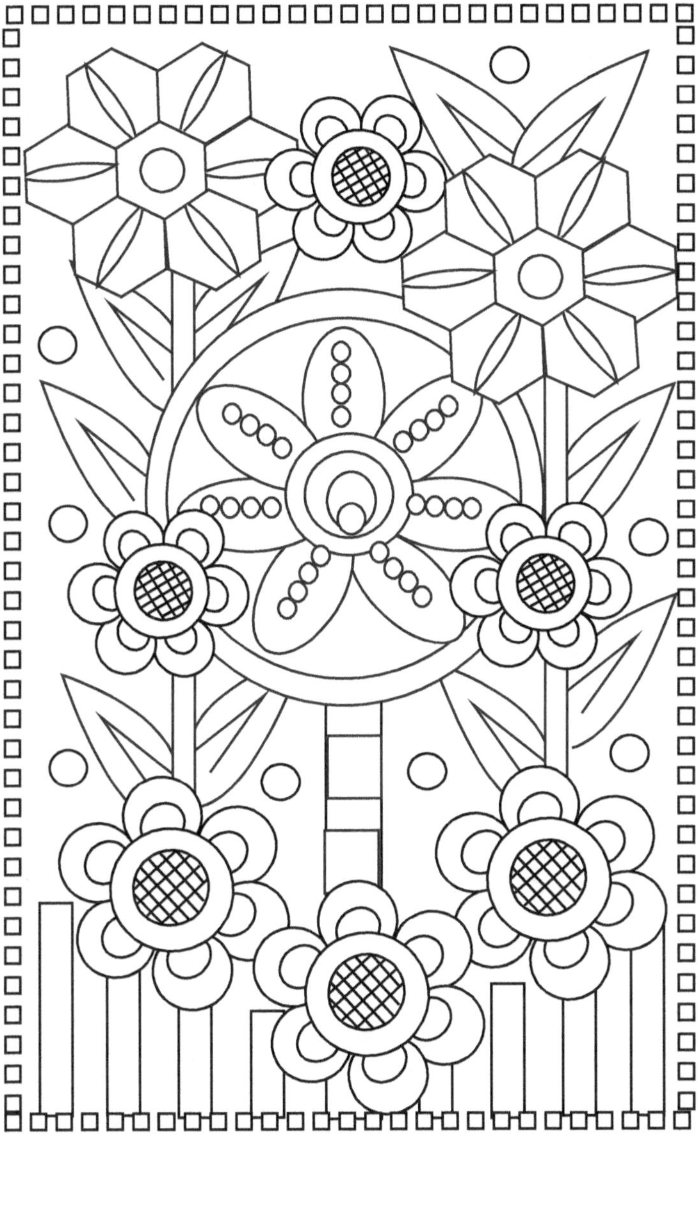

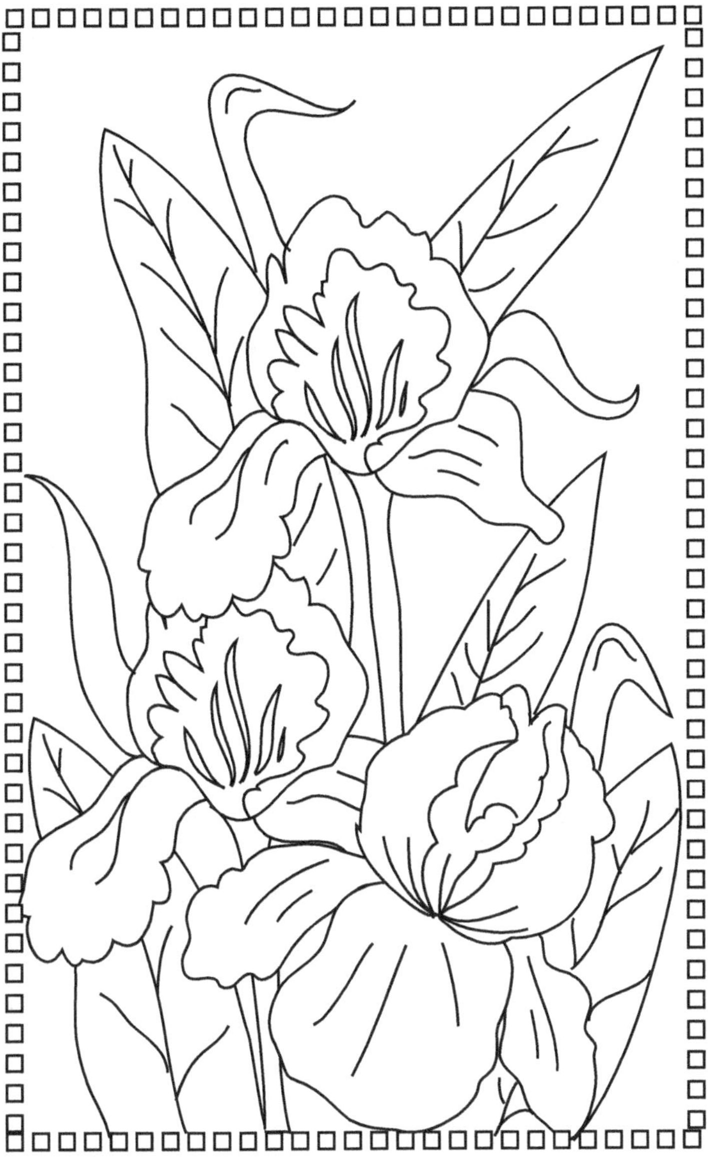

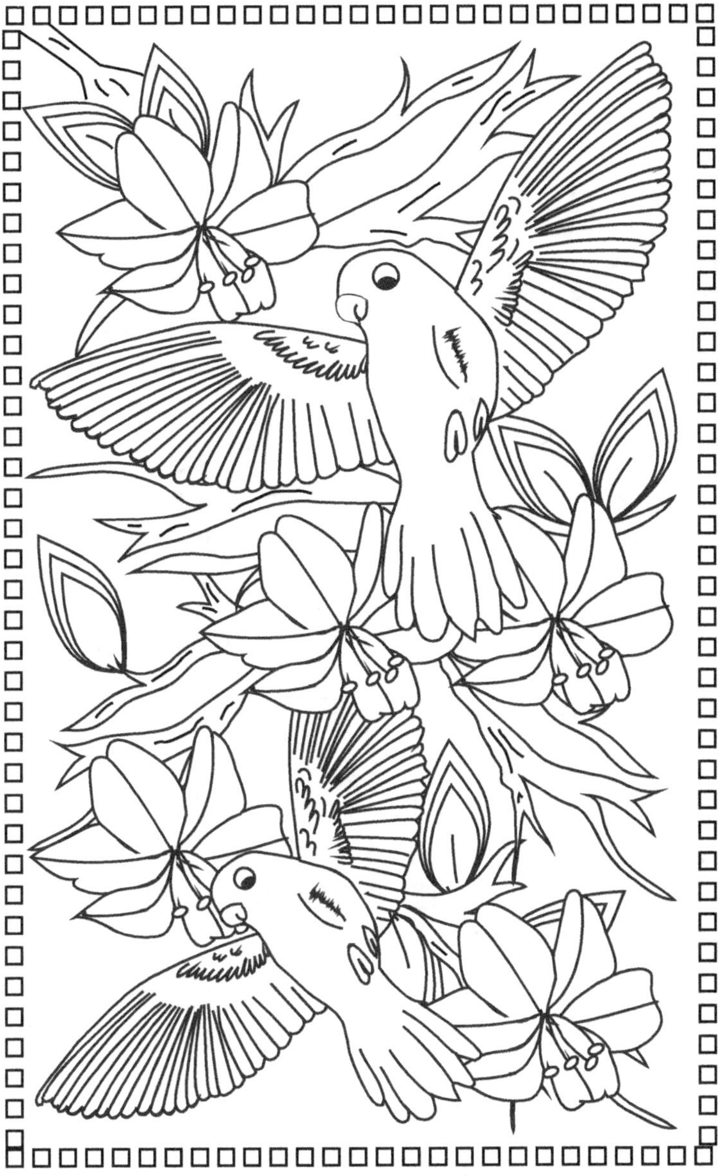

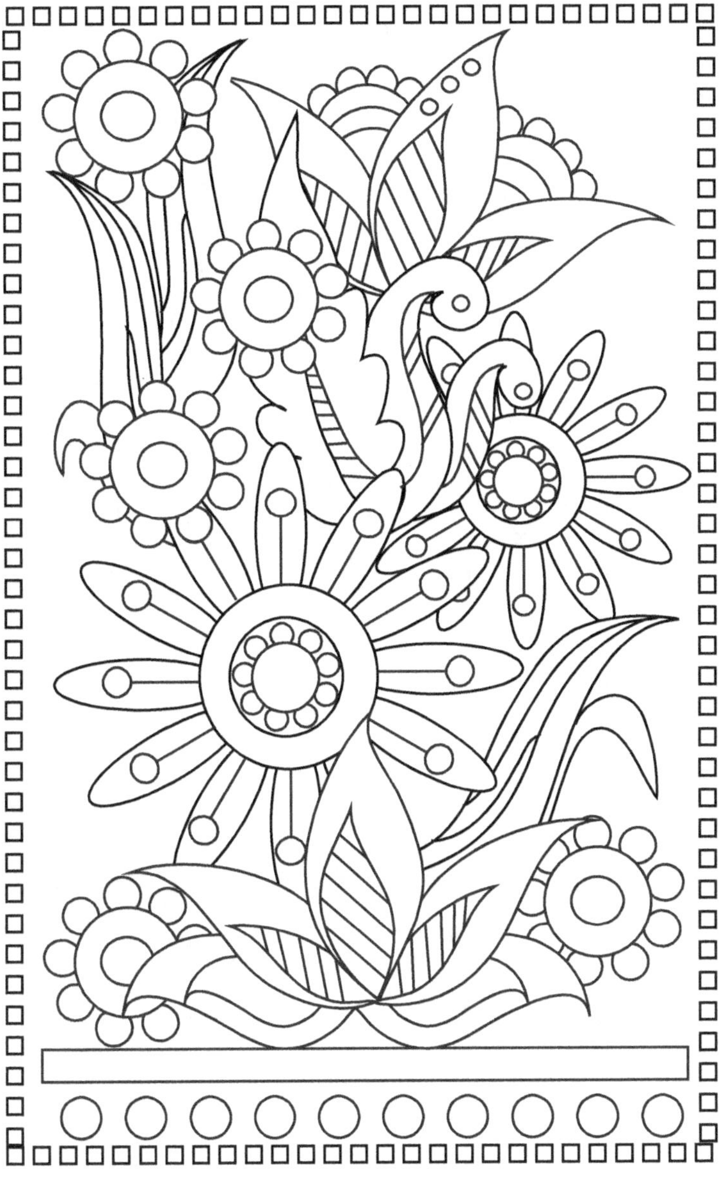

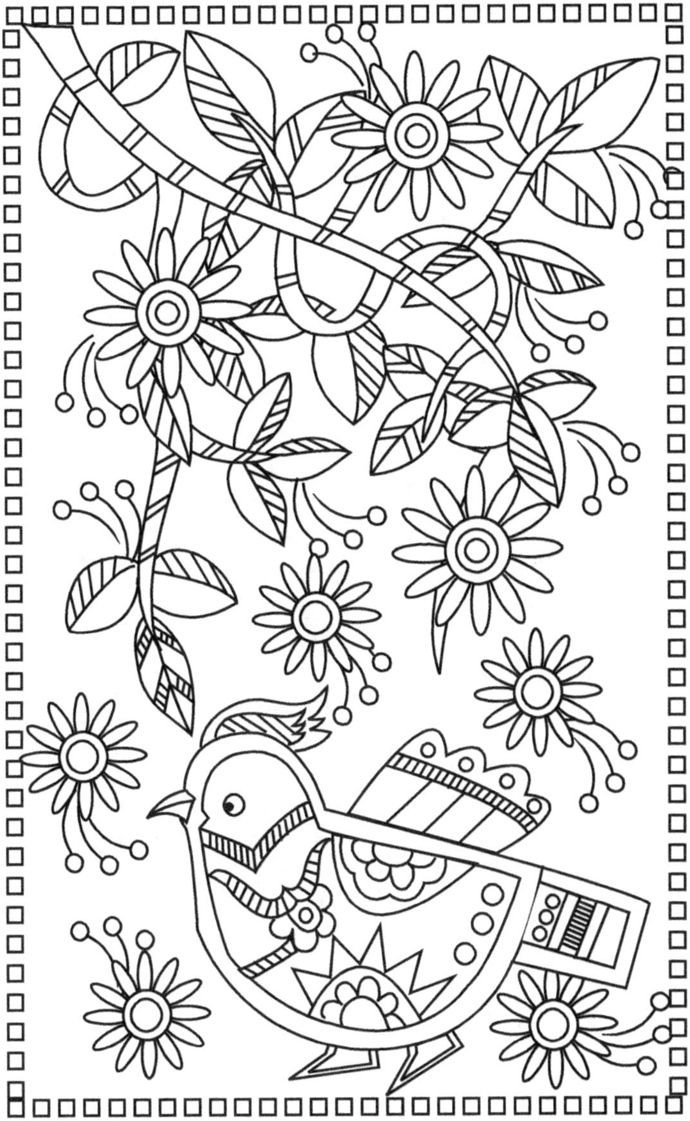

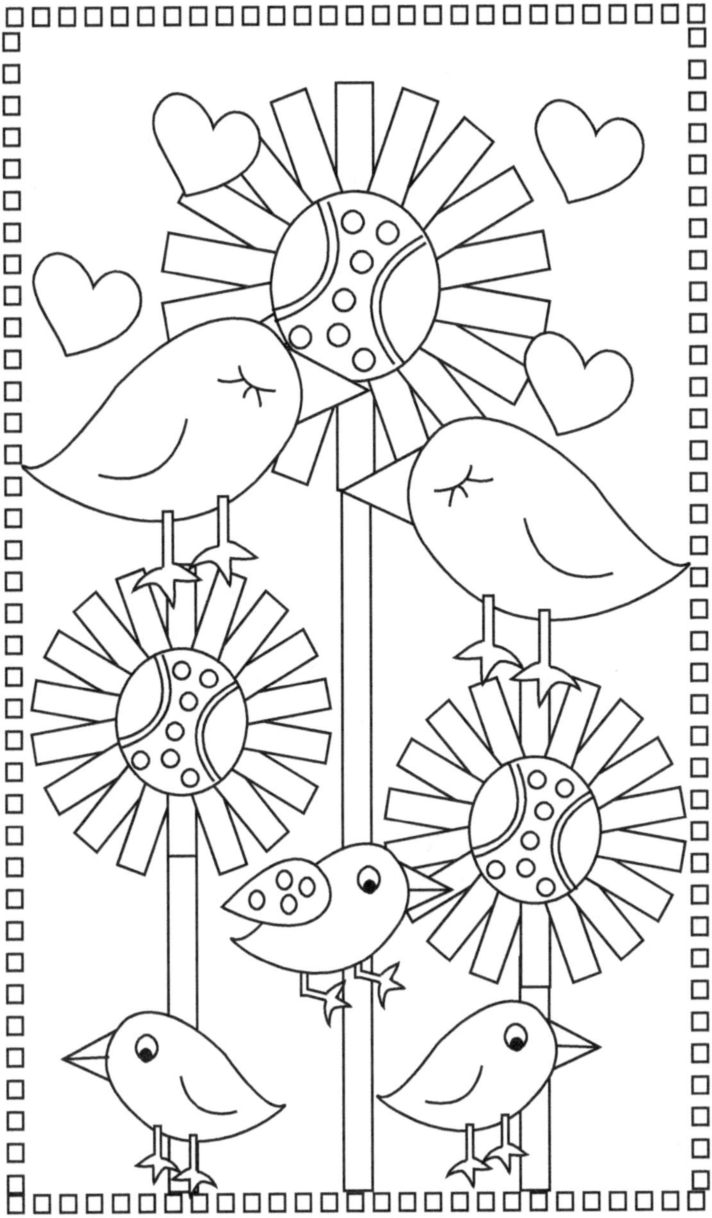

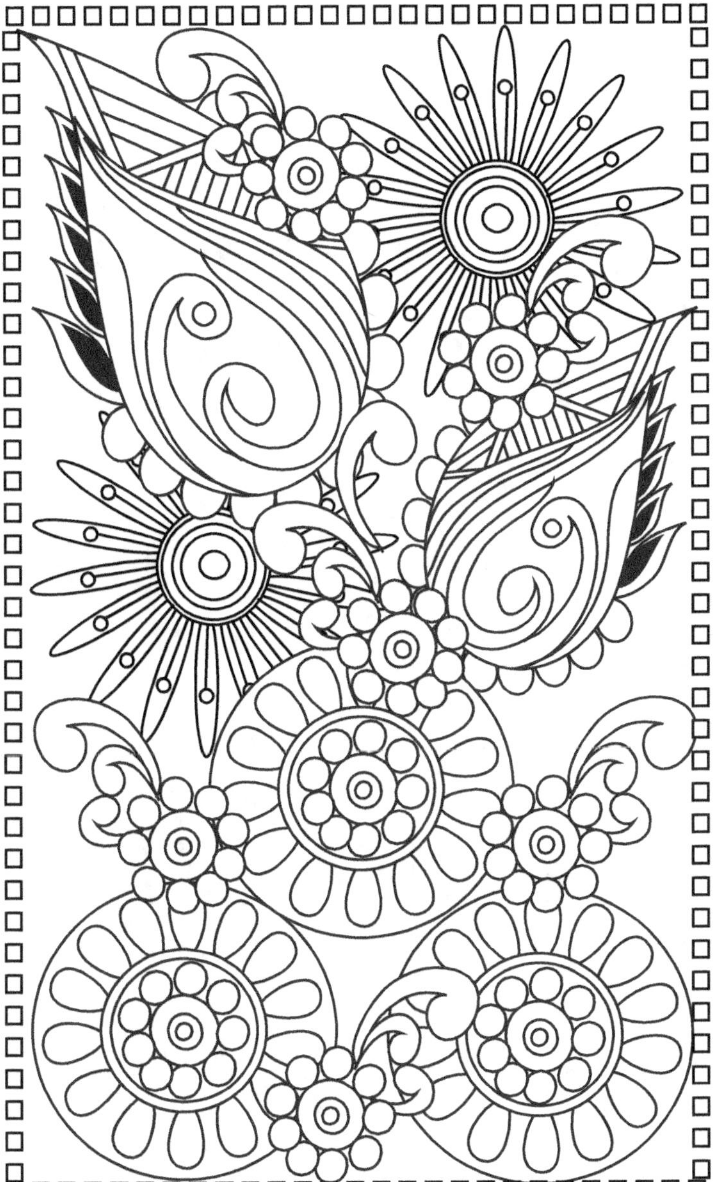

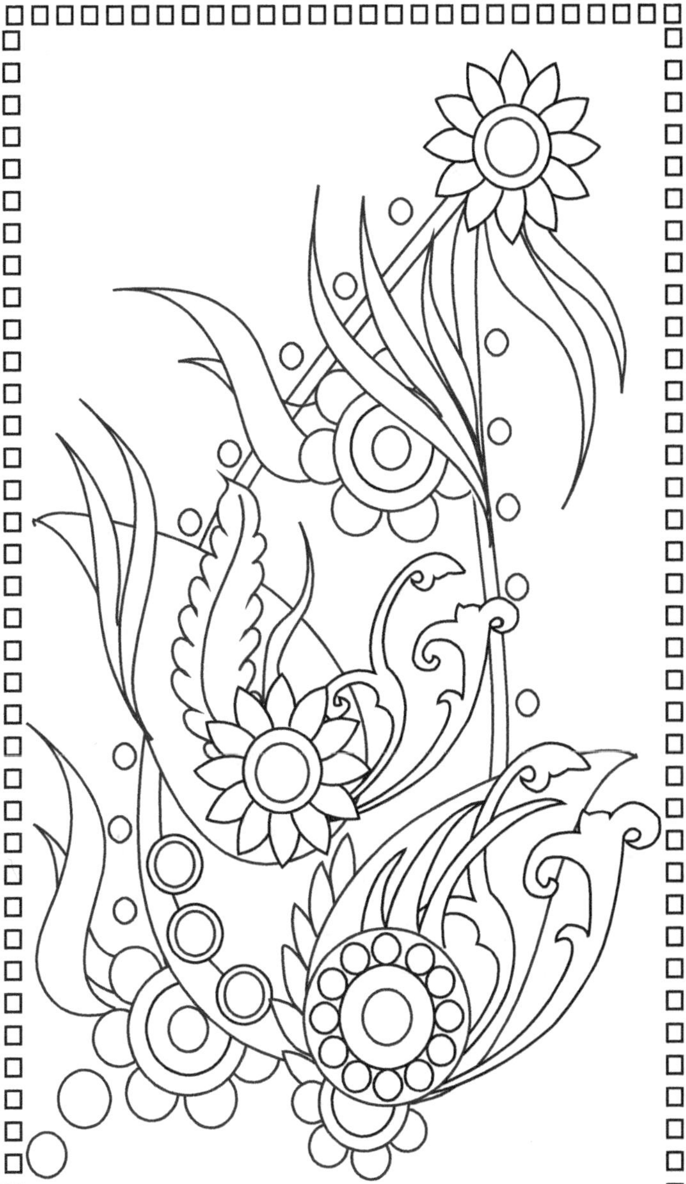

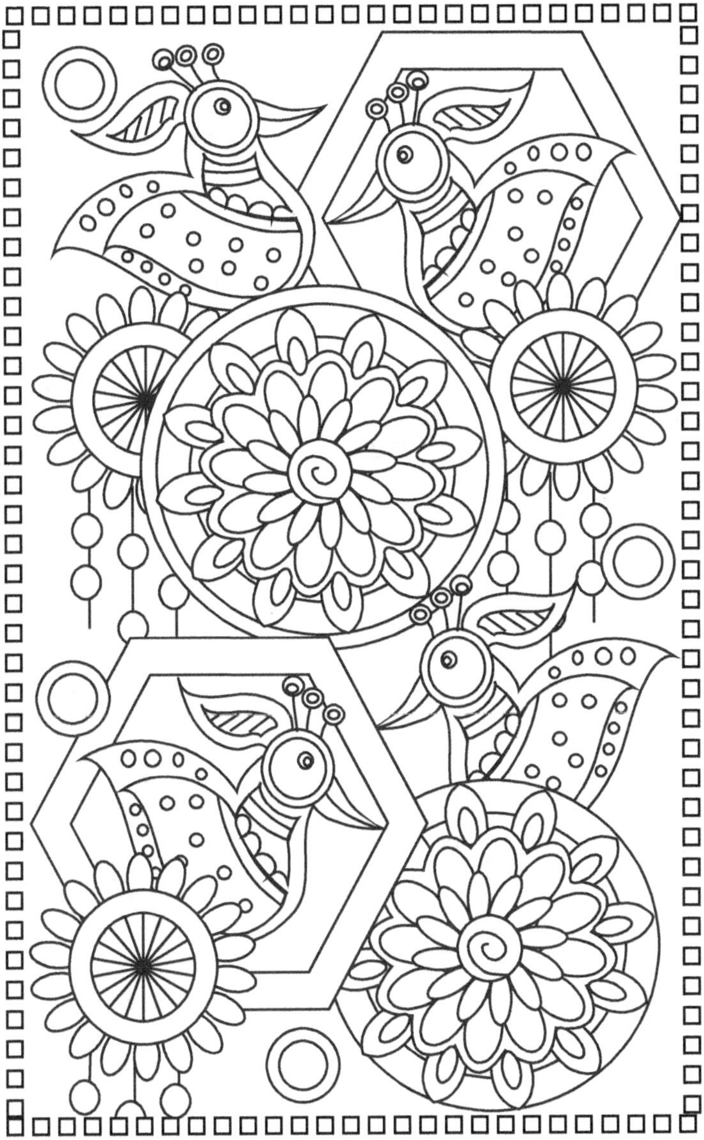

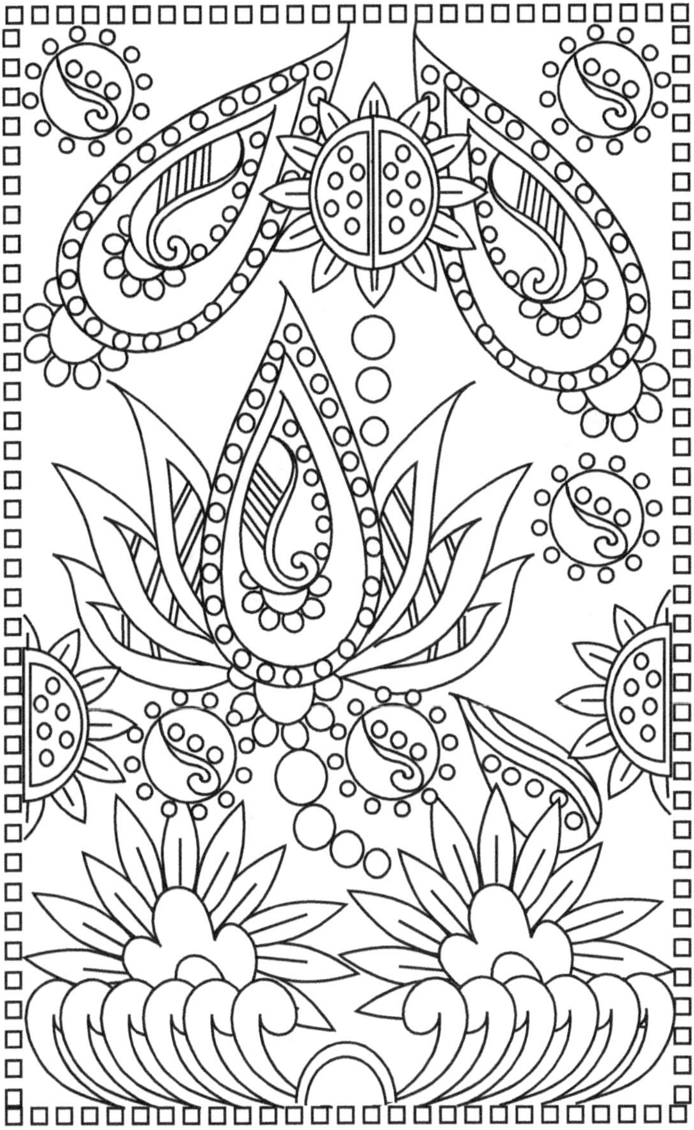

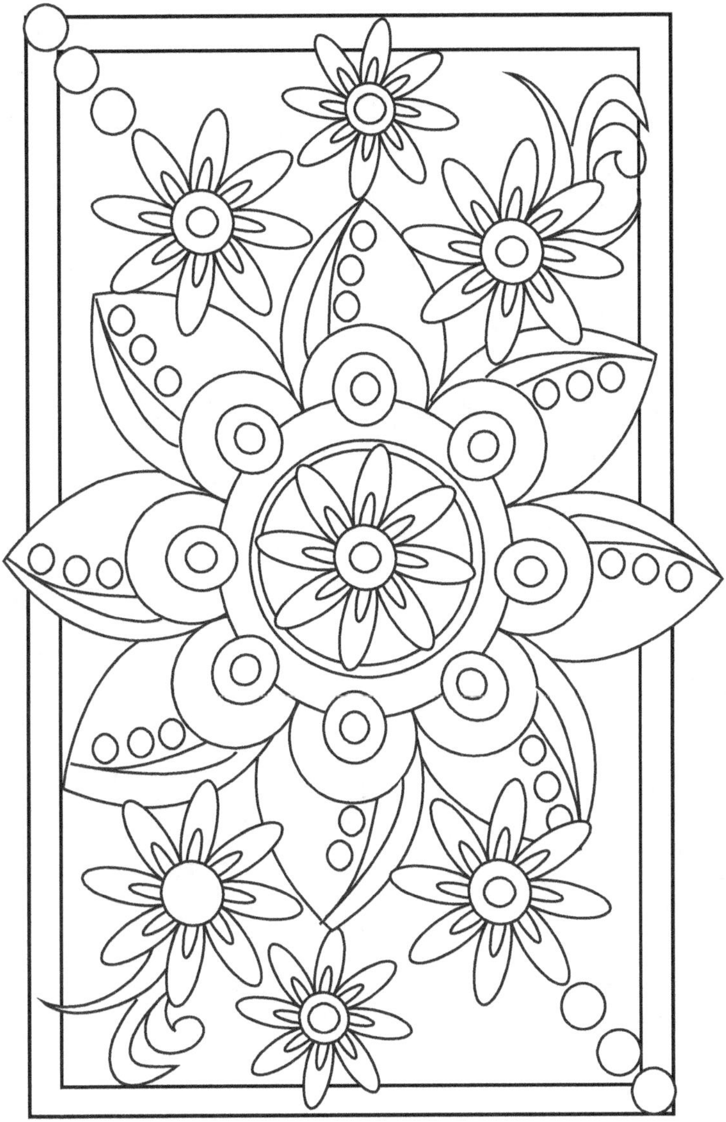

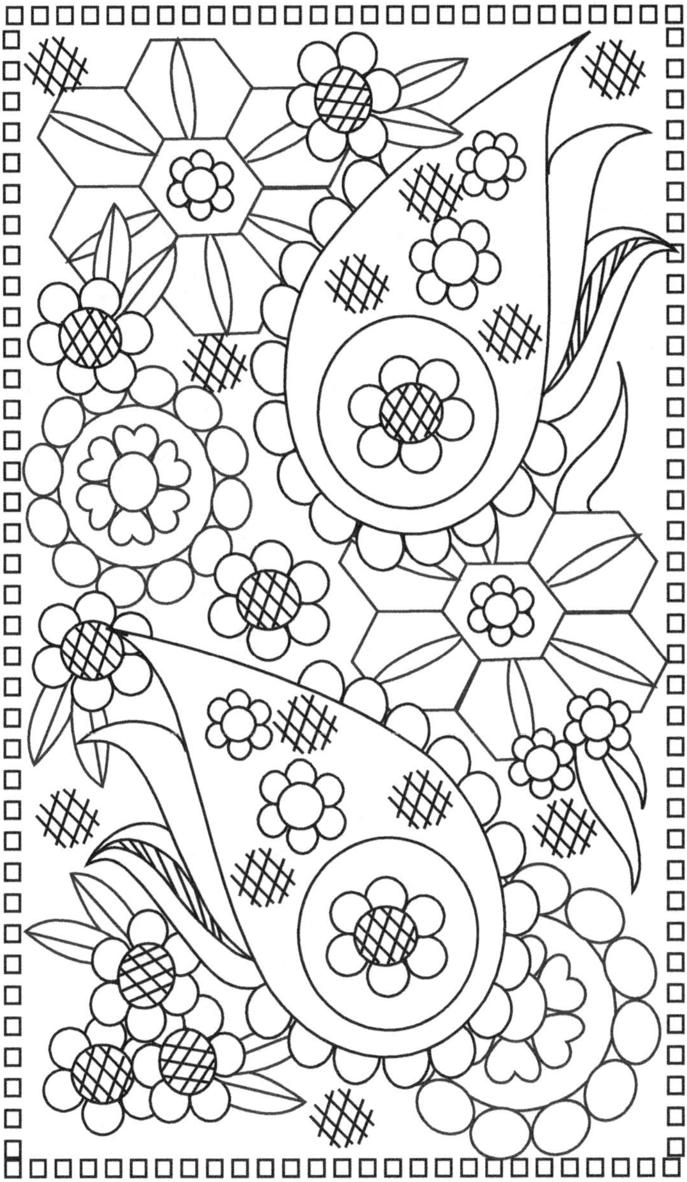

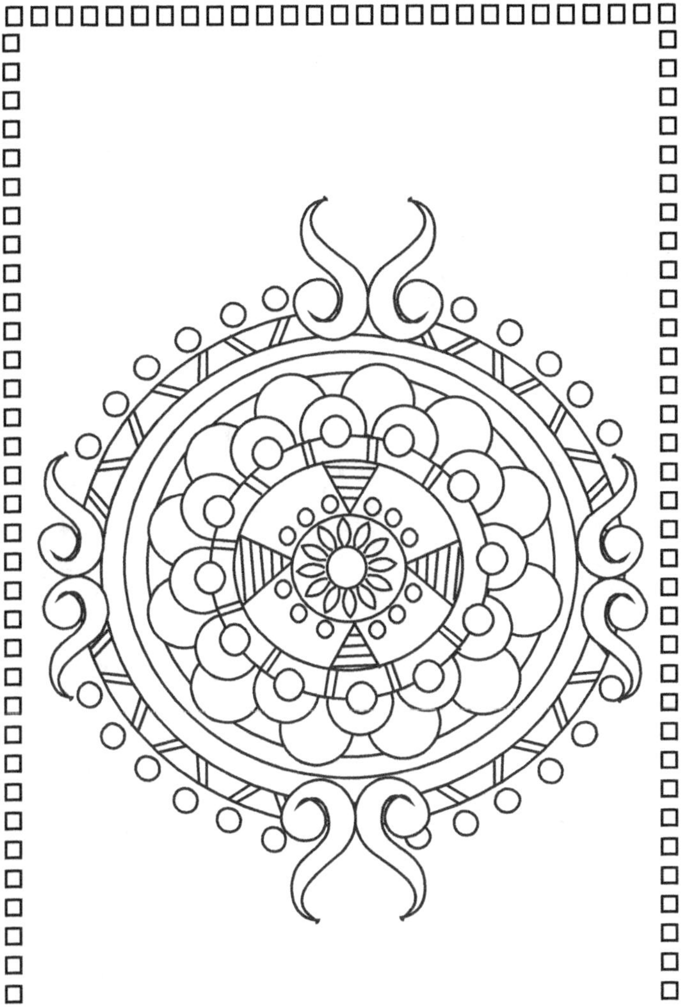

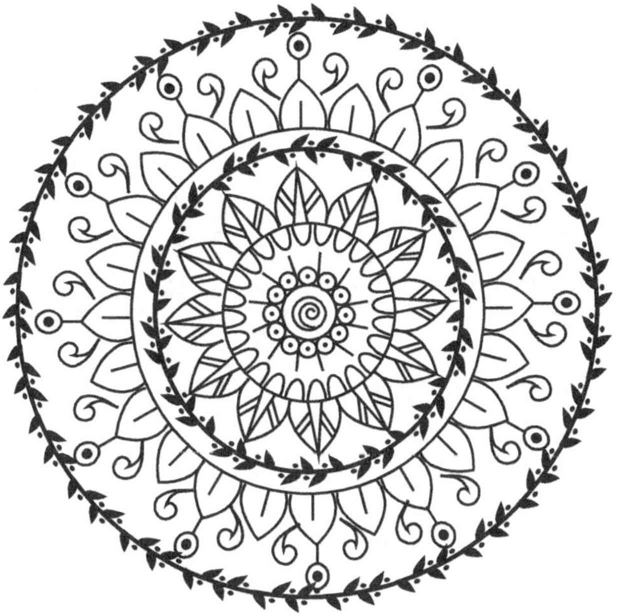

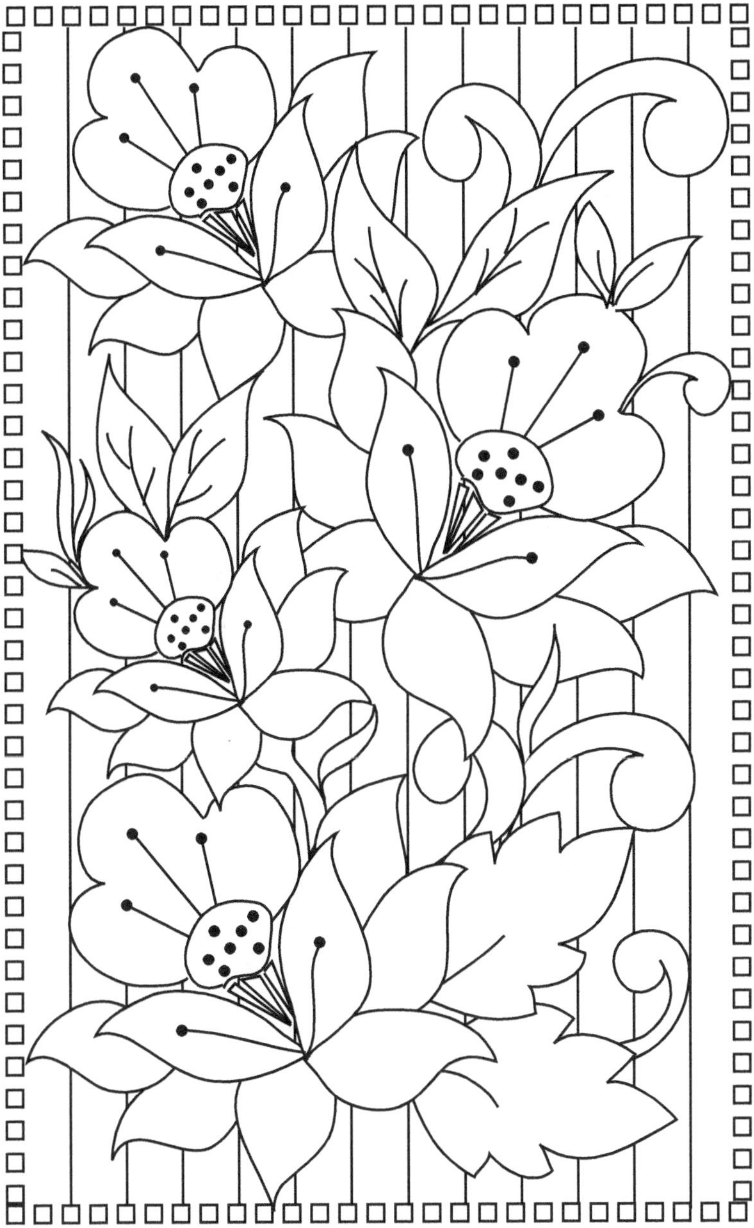

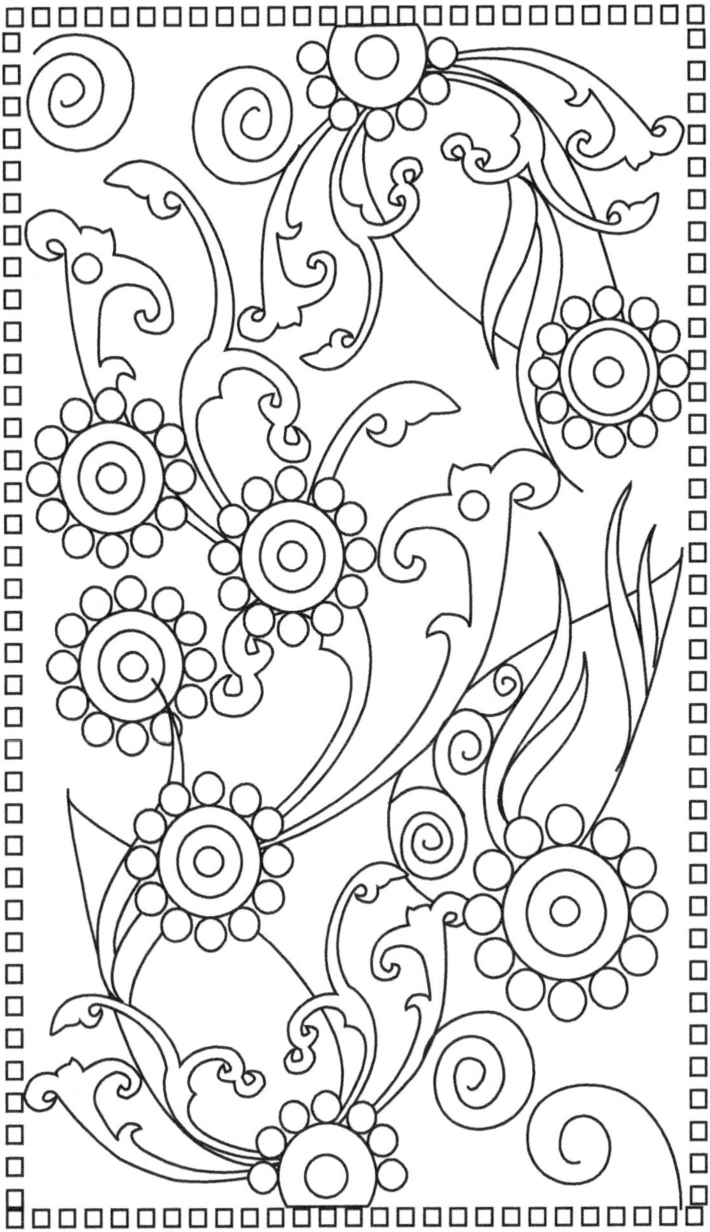

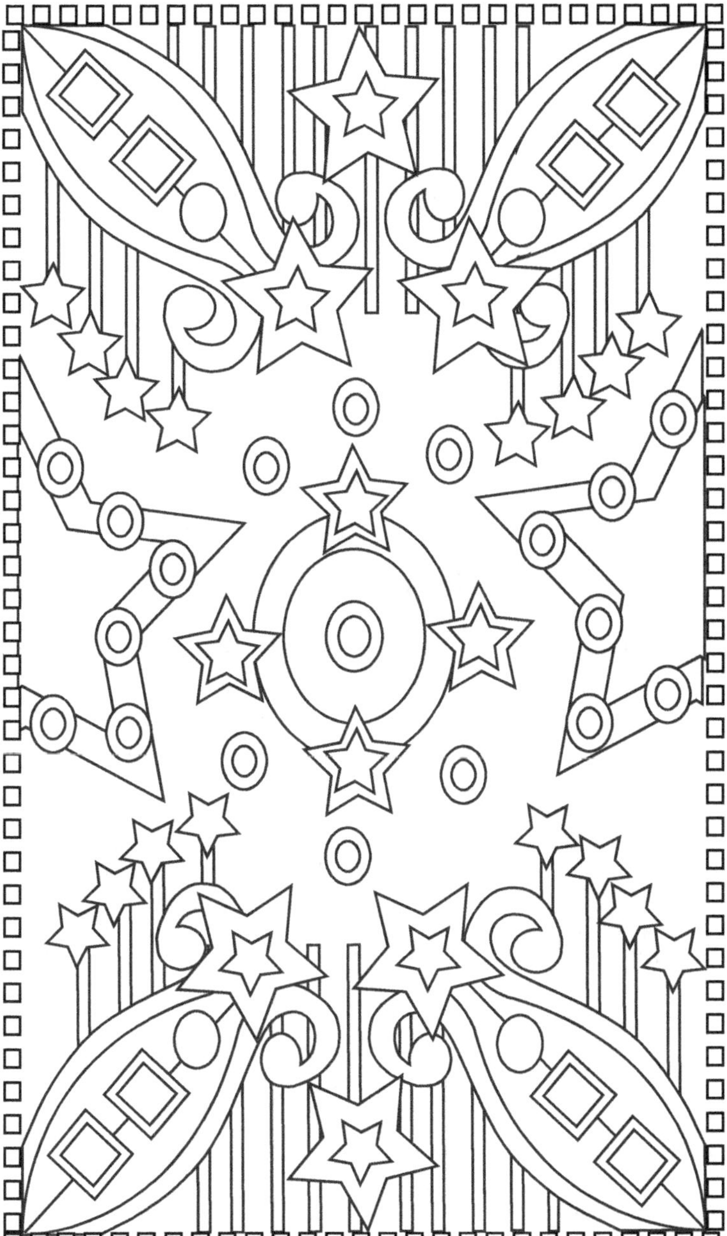

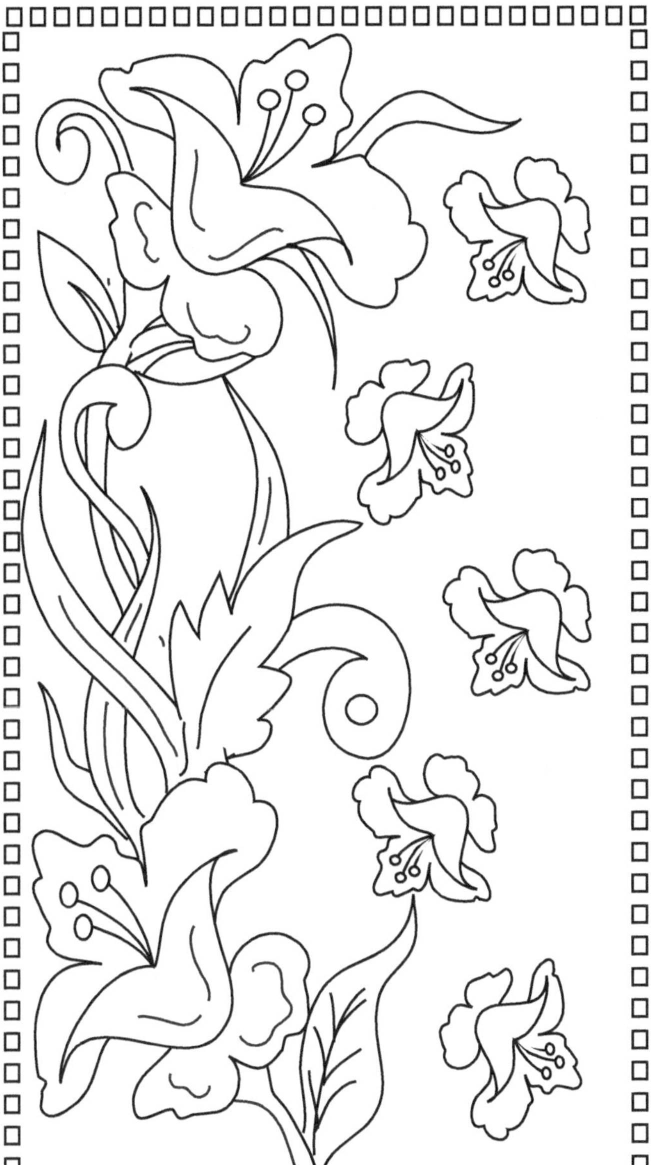

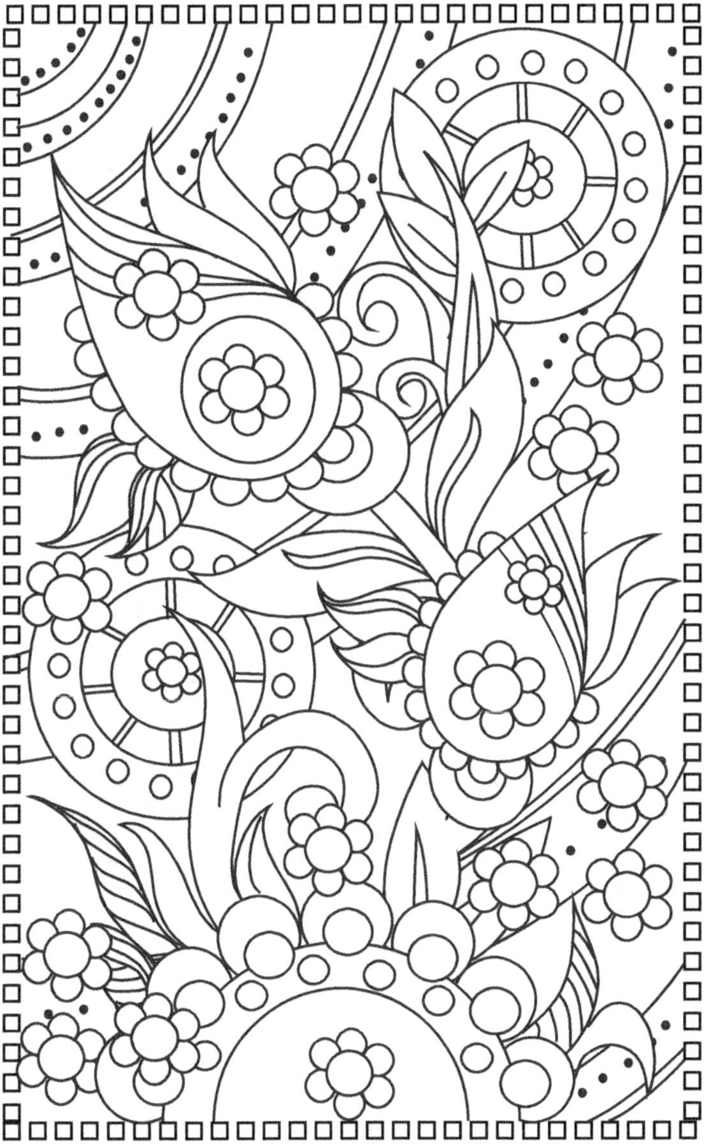

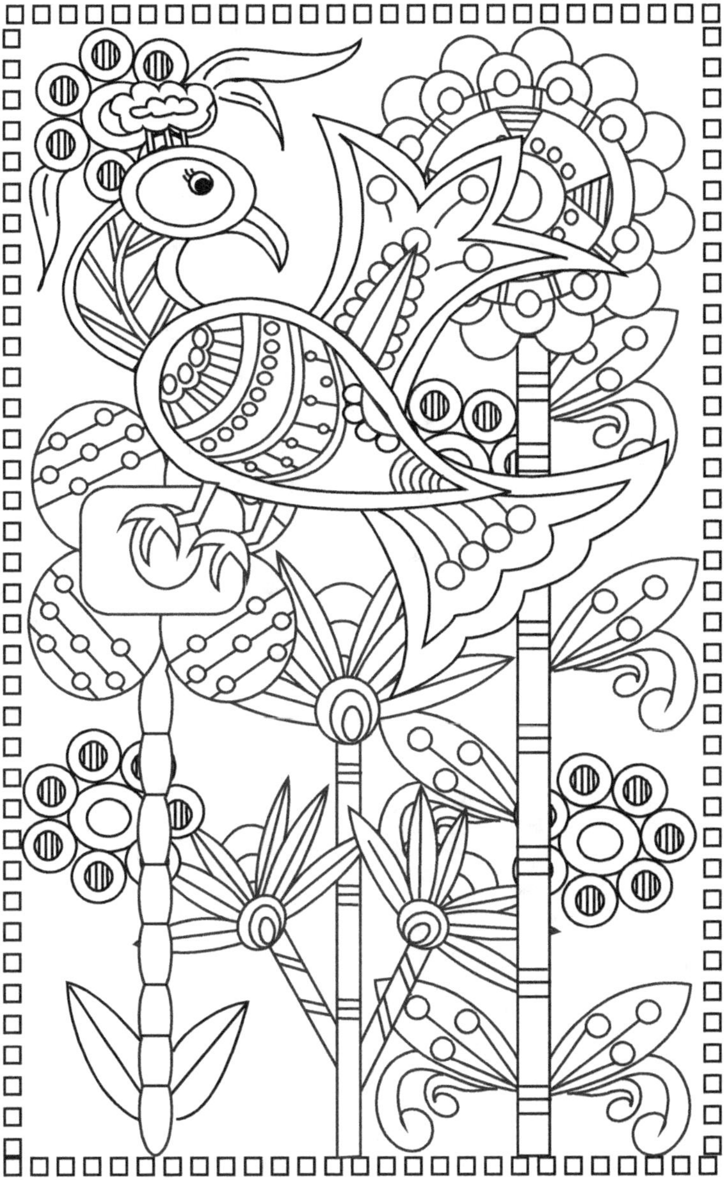

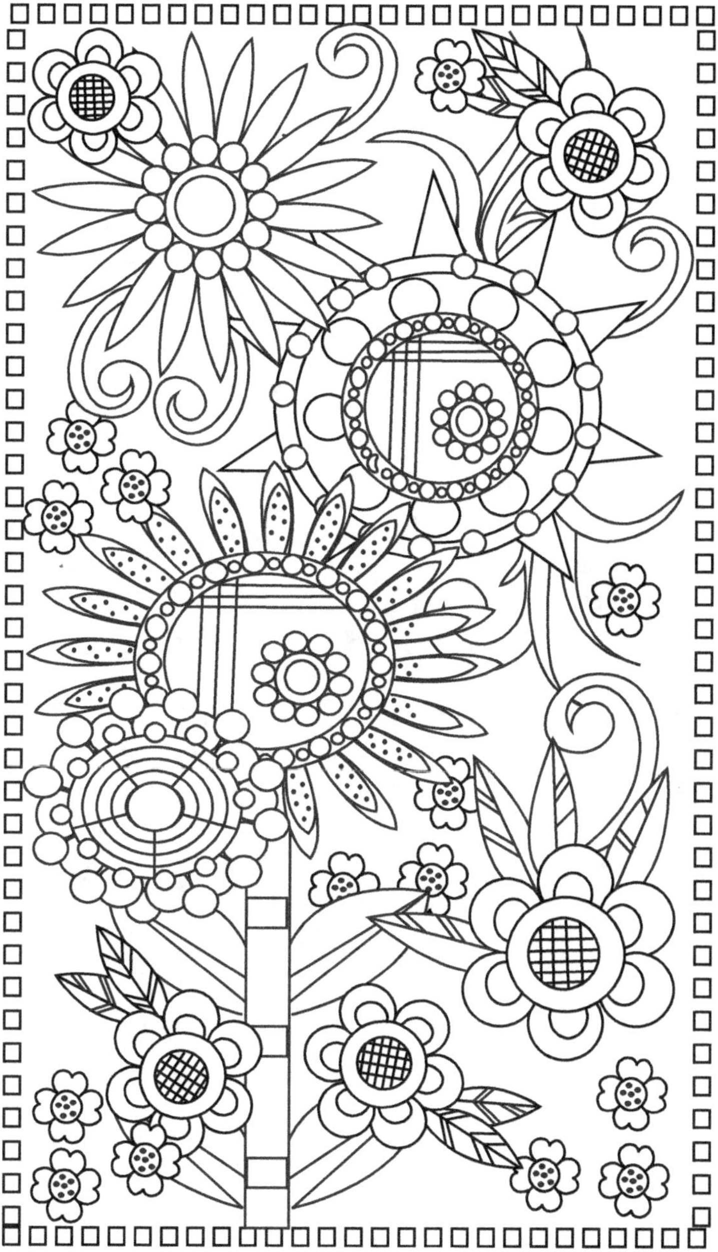

www.ingramcontent.com/pod-product-compliance
Lightning Source LLC
Chambersburg PA
CBHW071231220526
45468CB00002B/807
9781981485932